# CONTENTS

# INTRODUCTION

The first needles were made from cattle bone and used to sew animal hides together with lengths of sinew. Between then and now, people have sewn clothes for warmth, tents for shelter, sails for voyages of exploration, and flags for nations. It could be argued that a needle and thread in a skilled pair of hands has played as great a part in civilization as the invention of the wheel.

However, as everyday items around the home, needles and thread are mere clutter until we unlock their potential—together with our own—and master the basic techniques of sewing. This book has been prepared with beginners in mind, providing a step-by-step illustrated guide from threading a needle and learning basic stitches, to cutting and shaping fabric, and machine sewing with confidence. Whether you are just starting to sew or would like a refresher, this book aims to be a handy reference. Although this book was originally published in the UK, the technical terms and phrases throughout have been revised with a US audience in mind.

There are sections on all types of equipment; threads, fabrics and trimmings; how to read paper patterns; and what goes into making a garment. One complete part is devoted to the sewing machine, especially useful today when more and more households are investing in one. Other sections deal with smaller but important matters such as making repairs, using a seam gauge or inserting a zipper. Finally, the book contains three easy projects for you to practice your sewing skills, before embarking on the more ambitious ones you have planned.

# Sewing

## A beginner's step-by-step guide to stitching by hand and machine

**CHARLOTTE GERLINGS**

FOX CHAPEL
PUBLISHING

*To Thelma M. Nye, craft editor at B. T. Batsford Ltd for over thirty years and friend and advisor to many grateful authors and designers.*

Copyright © 2011, 2012 Arcturus Publishing Limited.

First Published in the United Kingdom by Arcturus Publishing Limited, 2011.
First published in North America in 2012, revised, by Fox Chapel Publishing, 1970 Broad Street, East Petersburg, PA 17520.

ISBN 978-1-56523-682-0

Front cover: Shutterstock
Back cover: Photograph reproduced by kind permission of Janome (www.janome.co.uk)

Illustrated by David Woodroffe
Projects devised by Sara Gerlings

Library of Congress Cataloging-in-Publication Data

Gerlings, Charlotte.
 Sewing / Charlotte Gerlings.
   p. cm. -- (Craft workbooks)
 ISBN 978-1-56523-682-0
 1.  Sewing.  I. Title.
 TT705.G47 2011
 646--dc23
                        2011024131

Fox Chapel Publishing, or to find a retailer near you, call toll-free 800-457-9112 or visit us at *www.FoxChapelPublishing.com*.

**Note to Authors:** We are always looking for talented authors to write new books. Please send a brief letter describing your idea to Acquisition Editor, 1970 Broad Street, East Petersburg, PA 17520.

Printed in China
First printing

# PART ONE:
# EQUIPMENT AND MATERIALS

## EQUIPMENT

A  Needles, pins, pin cushion(s)

B  Fabric and spools of thread

C  Thimble

D  Seam ripper

E  Dressmaking shears

F  Scissors

G  Embroidery scissors

H  Thread nippers

I  Pinking shears

J  Seam gauge

K  Transparent ruler

L  Fiberglass tape measure

M Tailor's chalk

N  Beeswax

O  Iron

P  Sleeveboard for dressmaking

Q  Sleeve roll and tailor's ham for dressmaking

R  Sewing machine

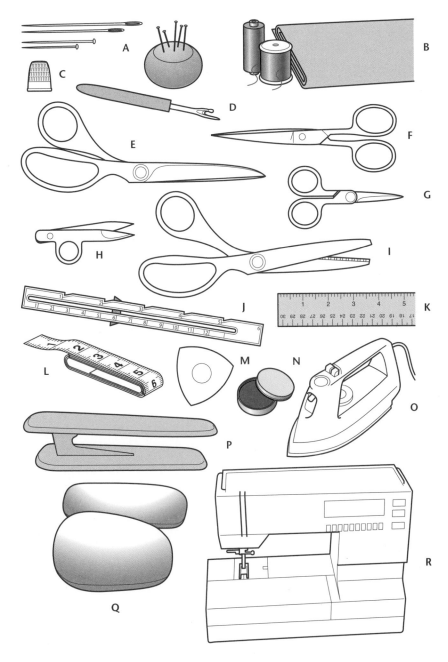

# NEEDLES, PINS AND CUTTING TOOLS

Hand sewing needles are manufactured in a wide range of lengths and thicknesses; the higher the number the finer the needle. Decide on the best needle for the job from the following basic list:

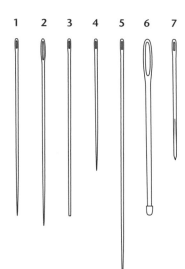

**1 Sharps** Medium-length and pointed, with a round eye, for general sewing with standard cotton or polyester thread.

**2 Crewel or embroidery** Pointed like sharps but with a long oval eye like a tapestry needle, for thicker or multiple threads.

**3 Blunt-tipped** Used for sewing knitted items, designed not to split the yarn.

**4 Betweens** Very short and sharp, with a small round eye. Used for fine stitching and quilting.

**5 Milliners or straws** Very long and thin, with a round eye, for decorative work and trims.

**6 Bodkin** Large, blunt-tipped, with an eye large enough to carry cord, elastic or ribbon through loops and casings.

**7 Glovers or leather** Sharp, with a 3-sided tip for piercing leather and PVC without tearing.

Most needles are nickel plated, although the quality varies. Gold- and platinum-plated needles don't discolor or rust but they are obviously more expensive. Keep and use a small emery pin cushion; the sand inside acts as an abrasive and polishes the needles and pins when they are pushed into it.

**Pins** made of hardened steel or brass will not rust; the smallest and finest are ideal for bridal and delicate fabrics. Colored glass or plastic heads make pins easier to see and handle. Keep a large, flat-based pin cushion handy for general work; a small dressmaker's wrist cushion is also useful when you are busy fitting garments or soft furnishings.

## Cutting tools (see p. 5)

Invest in the best quality shears and scissors that you can afford and don't allow anyone—including yourself—to dull them by cutting paper, cardboard, string or sticky tape. Look for blades secured with an adjustable screw rather than a rivet and have them professionally sharpened from time to time. Lefthanded scissors and shears are widely available through the internet.

**Dressmakers' and tailors' shears** have asymmetrical handles and long blades for cutting smoothly through fabric at a low angle on a flat surface. Chrome-plated steel shears are the most durable but fairly heavy. There are lighter versions in stainless steel with colored plastic handles.

**Pinking shears** make a scalloped or zigzag cut, producing a readymade seam finish that saves binding or oversewing.

**Sewing scissors** equipped with 6 in [15 cm] blades are the most useful size for your workbox. They have equal thumb and finger holes, and one pointed and one round-tipped blade for trimming and clipping seams.

**Embroidery scissors** are used not only by embroiderers but for precision cutting in other needlecrafts such as tapestry and quilting. The blades are 1¼–4 in [3–10 cm] in length and so sharply pointed that it is safest to keep them in a case.

**Thread nippers** have self-opening spring-action blades, making them quick and convenient to use, as well as being extremely precise. Made of steel and also available in a nickel, chrome or Teflon finish, the blades measure about 4½ in [11.5 cm].

A **seam ripper**, as its name implies, is the most effective tool for opening seams and removing machine stitching. Use with care because it is all too easy to pierce the surrounding fabric.

# THREAD

Choose a thread to suit your fabric so that sewing and laundering doesn't result in puckered seams, uneven shrinkage or broken fibers.

Silk thread (an animal fiber) is best for sewing woolens and silks. Cotton thread matches linen, cotton and rayon (all plant fibers); it has little give in it and is always best used on a tightly woven fabric. By contrast, nylon (polyamide) and polyester threads stretch and recover well so they are suited to stitching synthetic and knit fabrics; polyester will also stitch wool. Button thread is a useful heavy-duty thread for coat buttons and craftwork.

Colorwise, if you cannot match thread to fabric exactly, go for a shade darker; for a woven plaid, choose thread to match the main color.

Sewing threads are spun like knitting yarn by twisting two or more plys together; the tighter the twist, the smoother and stronger the thread will be. A loose twist produces a softer, lightweight thread like basting cotton, which breaks more easily.

Twist goes from left to right (S twist) or from right to left (Z twist).

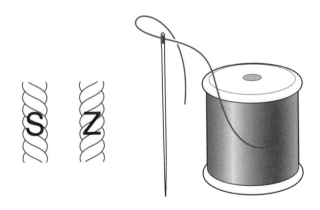

Standard sewing thread is spun with a Z twist, which makes it compatible with the workings of a lock-stitch sewing machine (pp. 10–11). Twist can also affect the way you thread a needle for hand sewing. Thread up with the free end as it comes off the spool and not only will it pass more easily through the eye of the needle, it won't tangle while you work.

Just like fabric and knitting yarns, sewing thread can be natural or man-made, or a combination of the two. Sewing with pure cotton has largely been replaced by cotton-covered polyester, where a polyester core provides strength and stretchability while the outer layer of mercerized cotton makes it smooth to work with.

We can still buy beautiful specialist threads of pure silk, linen, and even gold, which would have been familiar to needleworkers three or four hundred years ago. However, modern manufacturing processes have given us rayon or artificial silk (1910), nylon (1935), polyester (1941) and aluminum metal fiber (1946) at far more modest prices. What's more, textile engineers continue to design and test new threads for ever-developing markets—such as protective work wear and sport and leisure clothing.

Although most modern threads will tolerate machine washing, drying and ironing, do bear in mind that some rayons can shrink in a hot wash, while nylon and metallic threads will melt in direct contact with a hot iron.

If you do a lot of hand sewing and want to work more quickly and smoothly, draw your thread across a block of beeswax (p. 5) to prevent it from getting tangled or frayed. The wax treatment works well in conditions of high humidity and will kill any static electricity from polyester fleece and similar synthetics.

**Mercerized cotton has a finish applied to the plant fibers. They are immersed in sodium hydroxide (caustic soda) causing them to swell, untwist and shrink lengthwise. After rinsing, the fibers are left stronger, shinier and easier to dye.**

# FABRIC

Fabrics are manufactured from natural or man-made fibers, which are often mixed to combine their best qualities. For example, polyester cotton is equally comfortable but creases less than pure cotton; and the warmth of a woollen coat is complemented by the hard-wearing properties of nylon.

## Woven fabric

There are three types of weave on which all woven fabrics are based: plain, twill and satin. Each has different properties. If you plan to sew your own clothes, it is a good idea to start with a firmly constructed lightweight material such as plain weave cotton.

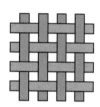

**1 Plain weave** is the simplest type, where alternate warp (lengthwise) threads go over one and under one of the weft (crosswise) threads. Muslin, calico, taffeta and poplin are all familiar examples.

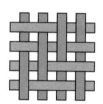

**2 Twill weave** interlaces warp and weft threads over and under two or more threads progressively. This produces a clear diagonal pattern on the surface of tough-wearing fabrics like drill, gabardine or denim.

**3 Satin weave** presents a smooth, compact surface created by long warp floats (usually of silk, cotton, acetate or rayon) that leave no weft visible; the reverse is matt. If the floats are formed by the weft threads, the fabric is called sateen. Either way, the glossy surface tends to snag.

## The grain

The grain of a fabric is the direction in which the warp and weft threads lie. The warp runs lengthwise, parallel to the selvage: this is the *lengthwise grain*. The weft follows the *crosswise grain*, at right angles to the selvage. Check the grain before laying out a paper pattern (pp.14–15). For garments, it usually runs from shoulder to hem; for curtains, it should run lengthwise from top to bottom.

## The bias

The bias lies along any diagonal line between the lengthwise and crosswise grains. True bias is at the 45 degree angle where you will get the maximum stretch. Strips cut on the bias are used for facings and bindings around necklines and armholes; they also form piping for soft furnishings.

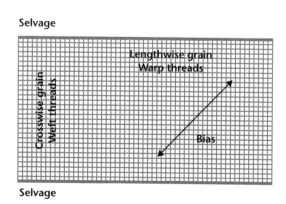

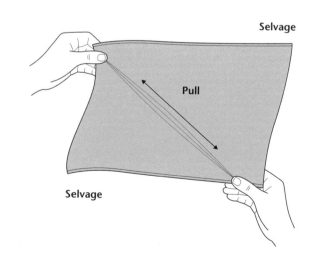

Jacquard weave combines plain, twill and satin weaving to produce damasks, brocades and tapestries. The technique was invented by Joseph Marie Jacquard in 1801, using a loom that wove intricate patterns controlled by a series of punched cards. Jacquard's revolutionary system later inspired mathematician Charles Babbage to develop the first mechanical computer.

**Tearing** Of the three, the plain weave will tear most easily because its threads are close together and cannot take the strain by bending, stretching or twisting. Plain weave tears in a straight line along the grain.

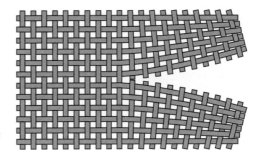

**Shrinkage** The tighter the weave, the less likely a fabric is to shrink, both during and after manufacture. The shop label will tell you if a fabric is washable or dry clean only. If it is not pre-shrunk you must do it yourself before cutting out. Immerse it in plain hot water for 30 minutes, then gently squeeze out, dry, and press if necessary.

# Knit fabric

Knit fabric is made from interlocking looped stitches; this means cut edges won't unravel and the material does not crease readily. Knits are not always stretchy; a firm jersey or fleece fabric is quite stable. By contrast, knits containing spandex fibers stretch lengthwise and crosswise, making them perfect for dance and sportswear. There are two main types of knit: weft knitting and warp knitting (sometimes called raschel).

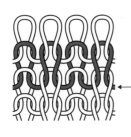

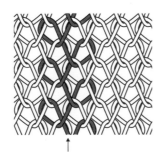

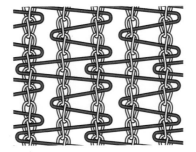

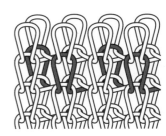

Weft thread course

Warp thread wale

**1 Weft knitted fabric** is produced like hand knitting, with loops formed by working a single yarn in courses or rows across the width of the fabric. It can be made on a variety of industrial or domestic knitting machines, and pieces can be shaped in the process. The course construction means it can be unravelled from one loose end.

**2 Warp knitting fabric** is formed by multiple strands of yarn making loops vertically in individual wales or columns. It uses a specialized machine to produce a fabric that stretches very little and won't ladder. Tricot and milanese for lingerie are typical products.

Warp-knitted end products include T-shirts, lace curtaining and blankets.

**Raschel** This type of warp knit has an open construction that can imitate lace and hand crochet, with heavy, textured inlaid threads held in place by a much finer yarn.

**Interlock** A smooth warp knit with closely interlocking stitches that allow it to stretch; it's typically used in the manufacture of underwear and casual clothes.

# THE SEWING MACHINE

Your single most important item of sewing equipment, a well-built sewing machine—whether it's a cast iron heirloom or the latest computerized model—will give you decades of service so long as it is properly used and maintained. Consult your owner's manual to learn how to use, operate, and care for your machine.

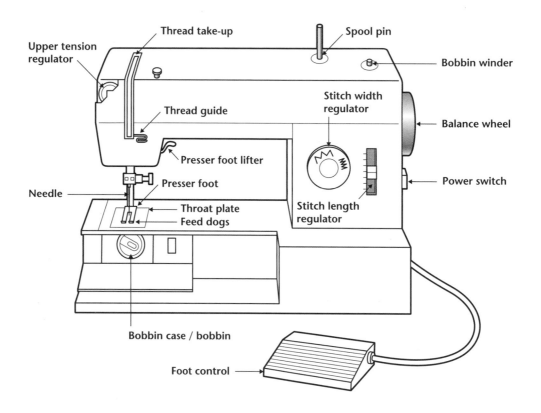

Buying new or secondhand, your choice will follow the kind of user you are. As a beginner or occasional sewer, look no further than a basic electric model (*shown above*) powered by an electric motor that drives the needle, bobbin and feed dogs, and operated by a foot pedal that controls sewing speed and fabric feed. It will sew different sizes of straight, hem, stretch and zigzag stitches selected at the twist of a dial, as well as button holes and a range of decorative stitches.

Computerized sewing machines (*see rear cover photograph*) are controlled by microchips and several internal motors, making them extremely versatile and a good deal more expensive. Operated using a touchpad and LCD display, with or without a foot or knee pedal, these are sophisticated machines that will even warn you when the bobbin is running out.

The fact that they can memorize and reproduce past tasks and offer hundreds of different stitches via downloads from a PC indicates that they are best suited to regular and professional or semi-professional users. If you plan to create a lot of garments, run an alteration and repair service, make soft furnishings or do complex embroidery, they are a worthwhile investment.

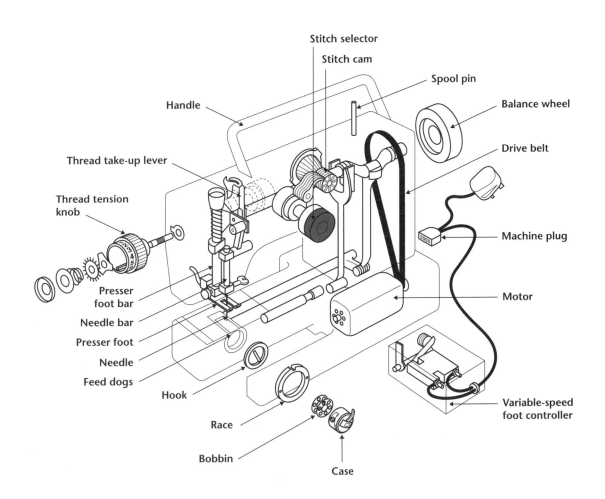

Stitch selector

Stitch cam

Spool pin

Handle

Balance wheel

Thread take-up lever

Drive belt

Thread tension knob

Machine plug

Presser foot bar

Motor

Needle bar

Presser foot

Needle

Feed dogs

Hook

Variable-speed foot controller

Race

Bobbin

Case

Prepare a list of the features that you want. Do you need a carrying case or will your machine be kept stationary on a table? Do you prefer a model with hand rather than foot control? Would you like it convertible from a flatbed to free arm access, which makes sewing sleeves easier?

Some basic requirements are: a good instruction manual; sturdy construction; bobbin is simple to wind and insert; threading up is straightforward; needles are easily changed; tension and pressure are adjustable; a lever or button for reverse stitching; variable speed control, including very slow; sews two or more layers of thick fabric without stalling; seam allowance marked on needle plate; light over needle area; thread cutter; minimal oiling, if any.

Garment-making on a large scale makes a serger worth considering. Widely used in industry, it combines machining, neatening and trimming seams in one operation. Overlockers operate with two, three or four threads producing looped stitches above and below the fabric edge; at the same time, a sharp cutter trims away the excess fabric.

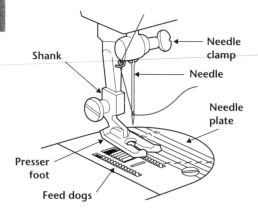

Shank

Needle clamp

Needle

Needle plate

Presser foot

Feed dogs

## Needle, presser foot, feed dogs, needle plate

General-purpose machine needles come in sizes 8–19. The finest will stitch delicates and the thickest will cope with tough fabrics like denim. Fit a ballpoint needle for knits or stretch fabrics. Needles will eventually go dull or break, so keep some spare and change them frequently. The presser foot holds the fabric flat against the feed dogs while the needle makes the stitch. The feed dogs have tiny metal teeth that move the fabric from front to back as the stitching proceeds. The needle plate fits over the feed dogs, covering the bobbin, with a hole for the tip of the needle to pass through.

## Machine feet

The shank of the foot (as seen on the straight-stitch foot below) attaches to the machine with a simple screw; newer machines have snap-on feet that save you time. There is a wide range of interchangeable feet, at least one for every stitch function. Here are five that form a useful basic kit.

    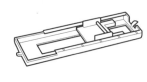

**1 Straight-stitch** The general purpose presser foot that comes ready to use on most machines.

**2 Zigzag** Has a horizontal slot to allow for the swing of the needle as it forms a zigzag with the thread.

**3 Zipper** Used to insert zippers and cording, or anywhere that the stitch line needs to run close. The foot can slide to left or right, and the needle operates in the tiny notch between the foot and the zipper.

**4 Walking/quilting** Uses teeth to feed upper and lower layers of fabric together evenly and avoid bunching. Ideal for vinyl, velvets, big plaids, and fabrics that tend to slip or stretch.

**5 Buttonhole slide** The button is placed in the carrier behind the needle and the stitching creates a buttonhole of the right length.

## General care and maintenance

When not in use, all machines should have a cover: dust is a big enemy. Regularly clean under the feed dogs and around the bobbin chase with a small brush—you will be surprised at the amount of lint that gathers there. Oil the machine only according to the maker's instructions and run scrap cotton fabric through afterward to soak up any excess. Avoid bent or broken needles by raising the needle high before removing work and don't drag on it while stitching. Sewing with a bent needle will cause it to hit the foot or needle plate and snap. Always raise the presser foot while threading the machine and lower it when you have finished work completely. As part of the power circuit, treat the foot control with care. Above all, switch power off before disconnecting any plugs or attempting cleaning or repairs.

Work at a table that is the right height for comfort and sit on an adjustable chair if possible. Facing a window will give the best light in the daytime. A pendant, standard or desk lamp can be used to direct extra light where you need it; fit daylight or halogen bulbs for a more natural effect.

# PAPER PATTERNS

## Taking measurements

**1 Height**  Stand flat against a wall and measure from top of head to floor

**2 Bust or chest**  Measure around the fullest part

**3 Waist**  Measure around the natural waistline; do not pull tight

**4 Hips**  Measure around the fullest part

**5 Shoulders**  Measure across back from point to point of shoulders

**6 Back–waist length**  Measure from nape of neck to waist

**7 Sleeve length**  Measure from center back neck, over point of shoulder and down slightly bent outer arm to wrist

**8 Torso**  Measure from center shoulder, under crotch, and back to shoulder

**9 Inside leg**  Measure from crotch to instep on inner leg

**10 Head**  Measure around widest part, across forehead

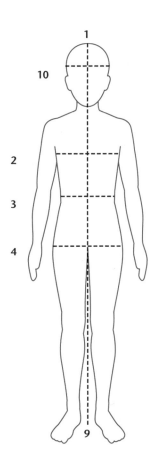

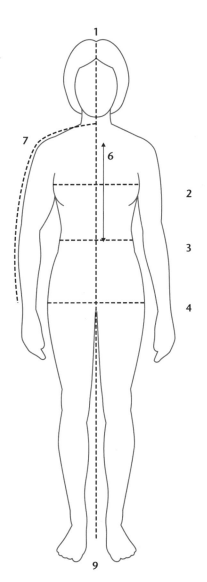

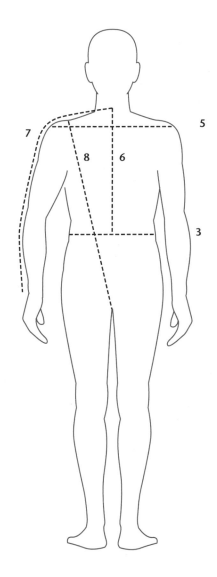

# Anatomy of a paper pattern

The front of the pattern shows a color illustration of the garment but the back of the envelope gives you all the essential information.

**Body measurements and size chart** →

| SIZES/TAILLES | 2 | 4 | 6 | 8 | 10 | 12 | 14 | 16 | 18 |
|---|---|---|---|---|---|---|---|---|---|
| Bust | 31½ | 32½ | 34 | 36 | 38 | 40 | 42 | 44 | 46 |
| Waist | 24 | 25 | 26½ | 28 | 30 | 32 | 34 | 37 | 39 |
| Hip | 33½ | 34½ | 36 | 38 | 40 | 42 | 44 | 46 | 48 |
| Poitrine | 80 | 83 | 87 | 92 | 97 | 102 | 107 | 112 | 117 |
| Taille | 61 | 64 | 67 | 71 | 76 | 81 | 87 | 94 | 99 |
| Hanches | 85 | 88 | 92 | 97 | 102 | 107 | 112 | 117 | 122 |

**Style number** →

# X852

# EASY/FACILE

**Garment description** →

**MISSES' TUNIC, SKIRT AND PANTS:** Pullover tunic A has collar, front facing, pockets and unfinished edges. Slim fitting skirt B and pants C sit 1" below waist and have concealed elastic waistlines.

**Notions** →

**NOTIONS: Skirt B, Pants C:** 1½ yds. of 1" Elastic.

**Suggested fabrics** →

**FABRICS: † Moderate Stretch Knits Only:** Lightweight Wool Jersey, Cotton Knit and Interlock. Unsuitable for obvious diagonals, plaids or stripes. Use nap yardages/layouts for pile, shaded or one-way design fabrics. *with nap. **without nap.

**TUNIQUE, JUPE ET PANTALON (J. femme):** Tunique à passer par la tête A avec col, parementure devant, poches et bord sans finition. Jupe B et pantalon C droits à 2.5 cm au-dessous de la taille, avec ligne de taille élastiquée cachée.

**MERCERIE: Jupe B, Pantalon C:** 1.4 m d'Elastique (2.5 cm).

**TISSUS: † Uniquement pour tricot à élasticité moyenne:** Jersey de laine fin, Tricot de coton et interlock. Rayures/grandes diagonales/écossais ne conviennent pas. Compte non tenu des raccords de rayures/carreaux. *avec sens. **sans sens.

**Combinations:** BB(2-4-6-8), F5(10-12-14-16-18)

**Séries:** BB(8-10-12-14), F5(16-18-20-22-24)

**Yardage required** →

| SIZES | 2 | 4 | 6 | 8 | 10 | 12 | 14 | 16 | 18 |
|---|---|---|---|---|---|---|---|---|---|
| **TUNIC A** | | | | | | | | | |
| 60"* | 2 | 2⅛ | 2⅛ | 2⅛ | 2⅛ | 2⅛ | 2⅛ | 2⅛ | 2¼ |
| **SKIRT B** | | | | | | | | | |
| 60"*, 7/8 yd. | | | | | | | | | |
| **PANTS C** | | | | | | | | | |
| 60"* | 1¼ | 1¼ | 1¼ | 1¼ | 1⅜ | 1½ | 2⅛ | 2⅛ | 2¼ |

| TAILLES | 8 | 10 | 12 | 14 | 16 | 18 | 20 | 22 | 24 |
|---|---|---|---|---|---|---|---|---|---|
| **TUNIQUE A** | | | | | | | | | |
| 150 cm* | 1.9 | 2.0 | 2.0 | 2.0 | 2.0 | 2.0 | 2.0 | 2.0 | 2.1 |
| **JUPE B** | | | | | | | | | |
| 150 cm*, 0.8 m | | | | | | | | | |
| **PANTALON C** | | | | | | | | | |
| 150cm* | 1.2 | 1.2 | 1.2 | 1.2 | 1.3 | 1.4 | 2.0 | 2.0 | 2.1 |

**Finished garment measurements** →

**Width, lower edge**

| | | | | | | | | | |
|---|---|---|---|---|---|---|---|---|---|
| Tunic A | 57½ | 58½ | 60 | 62 | 64 | 66 | 68 | 70 | 72 |
| Skirt B | 34 | 35 | 36½ | 38½ | 40½ | 42½ | 44½ | 46½ | 48½ |

**Largeur, à l'ourlet**

| | | | | | | | | | |
|---|---|---|---|---|---|---|---|---|---|
| Tunique A | 146 | 149 | 152 | 157 | 163 | 168 | 173 | 178 | 183 |
| Jupe B | 87 | 89 | 93 | 98 | 103 | 108 | 113 | 118 | 123 |

**Metric equivalents** →

**Width, each leg**

| | | | | | | | | | |
|---|---|---|---|---|---|---|---|---|---|
| Pants C | 16½ | 17 | 17½ | 18 | 18½ | 19 | 19½ | 20 | 20½ |

**Largeur, chaque jambe**

| | | | | | | | | | |
|---|---|---|---|---|---|---|---|---|---|
| Pantalon C | 42 | 43 | 45 | 46 | 47 | 48 | 50 | 51 | 52 |

**Back length from base of your neck**

| | | | | | | | | | |
|---|---|---|---|---|---|---|---|---|---|
| Tunic A | 29¾ | 30 | 30¼ | 30½ | 30¾ | 31 | 31¼ | 31½ | 31¾ |

**Longueur – dos, votre nuque à l'ourlet**

| | | | | | | | | | |
|---|---|---|---|---|---|---|---|---|---|
| Tunique A | 76 | 76 | 77 | 78 | 78 | 79 | 80 | 80 | 81 |

**Back length from waist**

Skirt B, 26"

**Longueur – dos, taille à ourlet**

Jupe B, 66 cm

**Side length from waist**

Pants C, 42"

**Longueur – côté, taille à ourlet**

Pantalon C, 107 cm

FRONT / DEVANT — A

FRONT / DEVANT — A B B

FRONT / DEVANT — C C

**Back view of garment** →

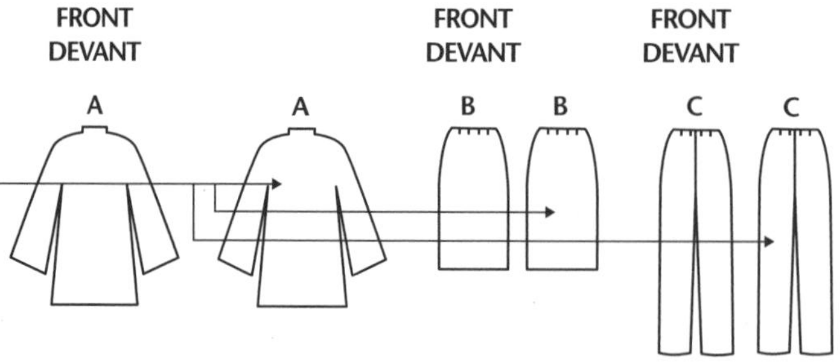

Inside the envelope you will find the printed pattern pieces together with the all-important sheet of directions. This sheet is a mini sewing tutorial, providing general instructions with explanations of pattern markings, the cutting layout, fabric preparation, a glossary of terms, and step-by-step sewing instructions.

A typical cutting layout is shown opposite. Fabric is manufactured in standard widths of 36–45 in (91–115 cm) for dress cottons; 52–60 in (137–152 cm) for polyester, wool, fleece and furnishing fabrics. Different layouts are provided for each width and whether the fabric has a directional nap like velvet, for example. Pattern shapes for interfacings and linings are included. The information is generally full and precise.

If you are working with a plaid fabric, wide stripes or a large repeat design you may not be able to cut out pattern pieces economically and will probably need to buy extra fabric for matching seams and openings. This extra amount should be mentioned on the pattern; if not, ask the shop assistant for advice.

## Cutting layout

The paper pattern pieces are arranged and pinned along the lengthwise grain of the fabric (pp. 8–9). The fabric is normally folded double but if a piece is to be cut from single thickness or on the crosswise grain it is clearly shown on the layout. The wrong side of the fabric is indicated by shading.

Pinning out is the stage at which you will take great care to match plaids, stripes and any other important features of the fabric, such as shot silk or taffeta. A shot fabric has warp and weft (filling) in two different colors, so the fabric appears to change from one to the other at different angles.

If you need to mark your fabric—for example, to locate the position of darts or buttonholes—use tailor's chalk (p. 5) or any of the special fabric marker pens available. Some have water-soluble ink and some will simply fade after a day or two; always follow the maker's instructions for use. The pens are not usually recommended for dry clean only fabric.

The notches on a paper pattern can either be cut out to stick up like a tab on the edge of the fabric or they can be cut the other way *into* the seam allowance, which is the reason they are called notches.

S/L stands for Selvage/Lisiere; F/P stands for Fold/Pliure. The numbers refer to the different pattern pieces.

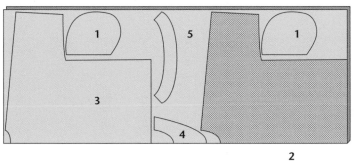

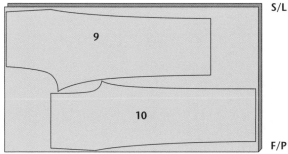

# NOTIONS

Notions are all those extras required to make the garment, apart from the fabric itself. Listed below are some typical notions. Buy them at the same time as the fabric to ensure a good color match if necessary.

A  Thread

B  Seam or bias tape

C  Elastic

D  Ribbon and lace

E  Buttons

F  Zipper

G  Poppers/snaps

H  Hooks and eyes

I  Hook and loop tape (Velcro)

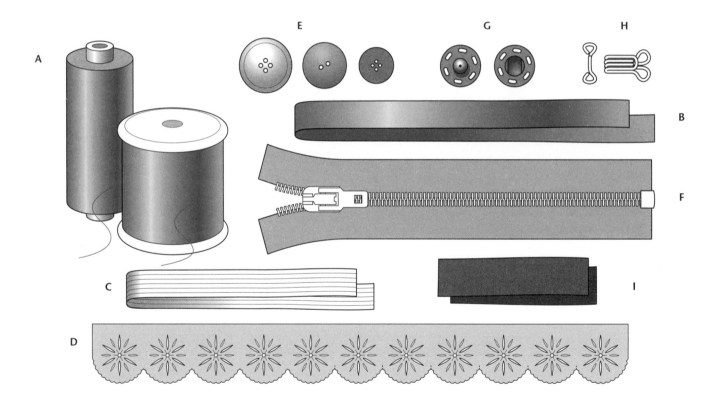

# PART TWO

# HAND SEWING METHODS AND TECHNIQUES

## THREADING A NEEDLE

If you have difficulty threading a needle for hand sewing, try using the needle threader that is supplied in sewing kits, or buy one from your fabric store.

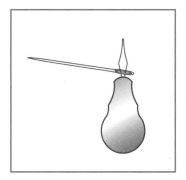

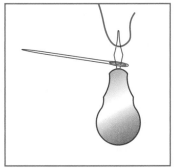

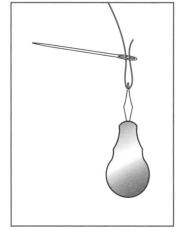

**3** Pull the wire loop back through the eye of the needle, bringing the thread with it. Remove the wire loop by pulling through the short end of the thread until you have just one thread in the eye of the needle and the wire loop becomes free.

**1** Holding the handle of the threader between thumb and forefinger, slide the empty wire loop through the eye of the needle.

**2** Place the sewing thread in the wire loop.

# STRAIGHT SEWING STITCHES

## Basting

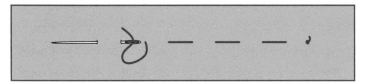

Holds fabric in position until final stitching is done. It's similar to running stitch but longer. Start with a knot, which you cut off when the time comes to remove the basting.

## Running stitch

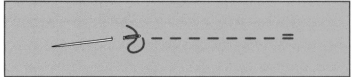

Simplest and most basic of stitches, used for seams and gathers. First secure thread with two small stitches on the spot. With needle at the front, push into fabric and out again in one move. Stitch and space should be of equal length. Fasten off with a back stitch.

## Back stitch

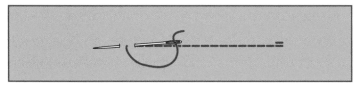

Imitates machine stitching. Begin exactly as for running stitch then stitch back over the first space. Needle out again at one stitch space ahead of the last stitch you made. Repeat with needle back in again at the point where the previous stitch ended.

## Blanket stitch

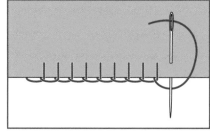

Used for neatening raw edges. Secured with a knot, bring needle through to front at stitch height and oversew fabric edge once, forming a loop. Pass needle through loop and pull tight against edge. Working from left to right, push needle into fabric again at same height. Pull needle forward through new loop to form a half-hitch. Tighten as before. Repeat in a row and fasten off with extra half-hitch around final loop.

# SEWING AN OPEN SEAM

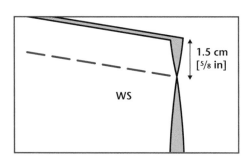

**1** Pin and baste right sides together before stitching a line of running or back stitch ⅝ in [1.5 cm] from the edge of the fabric. This margin is called the *seam allowance*.

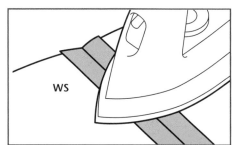

**2** Lay joined pieces out flat and press seam allowance open with an iron.

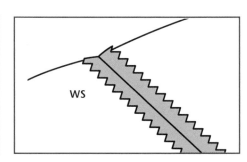

**3** Use pinking shears if necessary to neaten raw edges and prevent fraying. Alternatively, edges may be blanket-stitched or oversewn (p. 20).

# SEWING AN ENCASED SEAM

Encased seams, such as the French seam, enclose allowances so that no raw edges are left visible. They are suitable for unlined garments, lingerie and sheer fabrics that tend to fray. The double stitching stands up well to frequent wear and washing.

## Sewing a French seam by hand

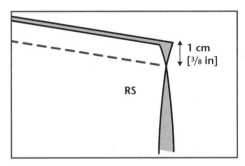

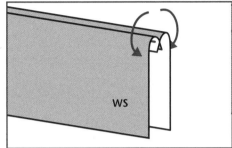

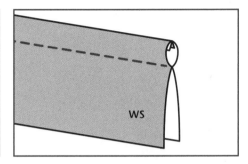

**1** Pin and baste *wrong* sides together before stitching a line of running or back stitch 3/8 in [1 cm] from the edge of the fabric.

**2** Trim both layers of seam allowance to 1/8 in [3 mm] and fold right sides of the fabric together down the stitched line. Press along the fold, enclosing the trimmed seam allowance.

**3** Stitch a second line 1/4 in [6 mm] from fold and press the finished seam to one side.

# CURVES AND CORNERS

## Clipping outer and inner curves

Curved seams naturally give rise to curved seam allowances, which have to be clipped to allow them to stretch or fold together neatly and lie flat.

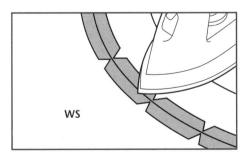

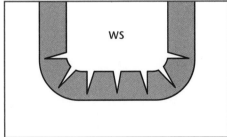

Necklines, armholes and pockets are all places where curves are clipped. If you have to clip down to the stitch line, be careful not to cut the stitching itself. If necessary afterward, use the *tip* of the iron to press the seam open over a curved surface such as a ham (p. 5) or pressing mitt.

Single cuts at regular intervals may be enough to ease together silk or cotton lawn, but to avoid bulking up on thicker fabrics, cut wedge-shaped notches into the seam allowance and remove the excess completely.

## Trimming corners

The same applies to corners, for example at the bottom of a bag or the ends of a waistband. Cut away excess fabric as close to the stitching as possible in order to turn out a sharp, right-angled corner. Use a crochet hook or knitting needle to help you—but nothing sharp that will damage the fabric.

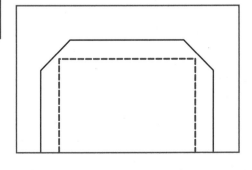

# MENDING

## Using straight stitches

Running stitch and back stitch are the ones to use for mending seams and casings (p. 22). Crossed seams—the point where four pieces of fabric are joined at the crotch or underarm of a garment—frequently need repair and to do this you must turn the garment inside out to reveal and replace the broken stitches. Begin and end $^3/_8$ in [1 cm] on either side of the break, where the stitching is still good. Where a line of top stitching has given way on a casing or on a flat fell seam (p. 39) you will easily mend that from the right side. Always secure the repair thread at start and finish with a back stitch; knots put unnecessary strain on threads and will show through fine fabric when ironed.

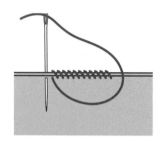
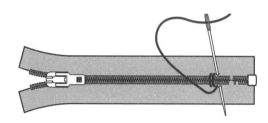
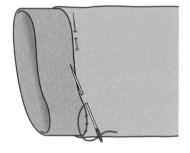

### Oversewing

Used for sewing two neatened edges together, for example when mending a tear, or attaching a tie-belt or length of trim to a garment. First secure thread with two small stitches on the spot and carry on with neat diagonal stitches equally spaced. This stitch can be done from left to right or vice versa.

### Oversewing a broken zipper

Provided the teeth are missing near the bottom of the zipper you can mend it by pulling the slider above the break and oversewing a new stop across both rows of teeth.

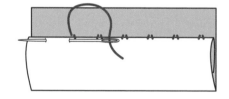

### Slip stitch

Used for stitching a folded edge invisibly to a flat surface. Catch up a few threads of flat fabric with your needle, enter fold and slide along inside for up to $^3/_8$ in [1 cm] before coming out again to make the next stitch.

### Repairing a sleeve lining

Slip stitch is ideal for repairing a sleeve lining at the cuff. If worn through, the lining can be completely undone around the inner cuff and turned up to hide the worn section. Pin the new fold and slip stitch the lining back into place.

# USING A SEAM/HEM GAUGE

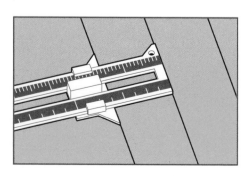

This is a 6 in [15 cm] gauge fitted with a sliding marker that allows you to set it on a fixed measurement. Use to ensure an even seam allowance or hem, or to measure pleats and buttonholes accurately.

# HEMMING

## Turning a hem

Hemming is frequently done by hand, even when the rest of a garment is machine stitched.

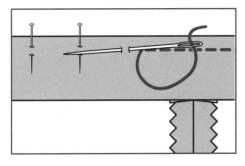

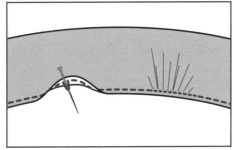

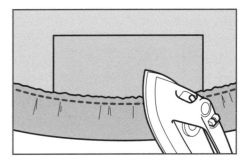

**1** Let the garment hang for a day before pinning up the hem, then baste the lower edge and turn the raw edge over at the top, ready to stitch. If the fabric is fraying or too thick, sew tape around the right side of the raw edge and hem stitch on to that (p. 24).

**2** For a flared or circular hem, ease fullness with running stitch around the top edge. Pull up regular groups of gathers using a pin, then baste in preparation for stitching. Alternatively, attach bias tape (p. 24) after gathering.

**3** Steam pressing heavy woolen fabric helps to reduce hem fullness. Use cloth or thick paper to avoid making a ridge on the front of the fabric. Press very lightly and lift the iron clear—never drag it across damp fabric.

## Hemming stitch

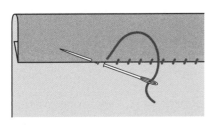

The second turn of the hem should be narrower than the first, about ¼–³/₈ in [7–10 mm]. Secure thread with two small stitches on the edge of this fold. Begin hemming by picking up two or three threads of the main fabric before passing needle up to catch the fold again. This stitch can be worked from right or left.

## Slip hemming

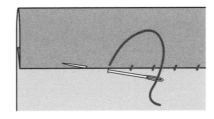

Similar to slip stitch (p.20). Pick up a few threads of fabric with the needle, enter fold and slide along inside for up to ³/₈ in [1 cm] before emerging to make the next stitch.

## Herringbone (Catchstitch) flat hem

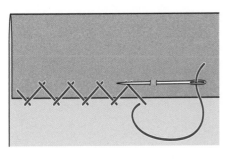

Secures hems on thick, non-fraying fabrics where no second turning is made. It is basically a large cross stitch formed by making a back stitch alternately in each layer of fabric.

## Rolled hem

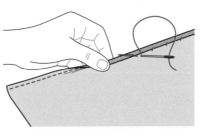

For delicate fabrics: first stitch along a marked hemline with a fine needle. Trim to within ¼ in [5 mm] of that line and, between thumb and forefinger, start rolling the raw edge over the stitching. Insert your needle through the roll, catch a thread or two in the main fabric and slide the needle into the roll again. Every few stitches, draw up thread to secure roll.

# CASINGS

A casing is a tube for elastic, cord or ribbon. Stretch waistbands, scrunchies and shoebags all use casings. In home furnishing, the casing may take a curtain rod or wire. Make it deep enough and you can stitch a second line to hold the rod *and* create a frilled curtain top.

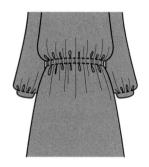

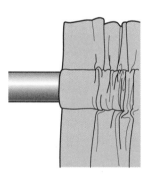

## Making a casing

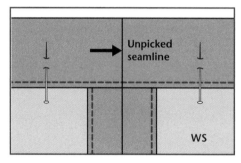

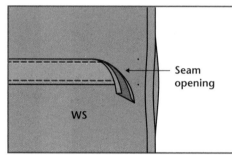

1 Fold fabric over twice, like a hem. Pin, then stitch. If hand sewing, use back stitch for strength because a casing gets considerable wear. To leave a gap for drawstrings (on a shoebag, for example) undo both side seams above the horizontal stitch line; leave the seam allowance turned inside.

2 Alternatively, create a channel with straight tape. Sewn on to the wrong side of the fabric, it should be a little wider than the elastic, ribbon or cord going through it. Make use of any seam openings to thread the elastic etc., but close them separately without blocking the channel.

## Threading the casing

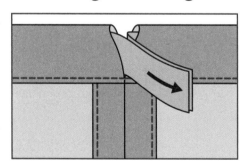

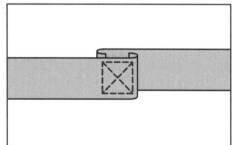

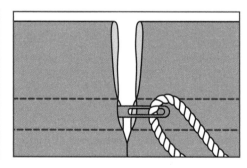

1 Calculate how much elastic you need by stretching it around the waist, wrist etc. and allow extra for adjustment and sewing the ends. It will be shorter than the casing, so safety-pin the free end to the fabric before threading; the casing will gather up as you go. Level the ends outside the casing when threading is done, pin together and check for fit.

2 Trim any excess if necessary, then join the elastic as shown, unless it is very narrow and you are unable to fold the ends. Stitch a square and/or a cross for a really firm hold. The waistband, cuff etc. can then be closed.

3 To fit a two-way drawstring, buy enough cord to go twice round the top of the bag with about 12 in [30 cm] to spare. The casing should have a gap in the seam on each side. Cut the cord in half and with a bodkin, thread each half right around the casing, starting and finishing on opposite sides. Knot the cord ends together tightly; pull both sides at once to close the bag.

# PROJECT: DRAWSTRING FAVOR BAG

This little bag measures 4 x 7 in [10 x 18 cm] and can be hand sewn using organza and ribbons to hold favors for parties, weddings or naming ceremonies. Made from muslin or fine cotton lawn, it could also contain a sachet of lavender or aromatic cedar wood for a clothes cupboard or drawer. The same pattern may be scaled up to the appropriate size for laundry, shoes or toys, using any suitable fabric.

To make a favor bag, you will need:
• a piece of organza cut to 5¼ x 18 in [13 x 46 cm]
• a 10 in [25 cm] length of silk, satin or nylon ribbon ⅝ in [15 mm] wide for the external casing
• 26 in [65 cm] of matching ribbon ¼ in [7 mm] wide for the two-way drawstring. Alternatively, use the same amount of thin silky cord

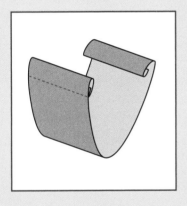

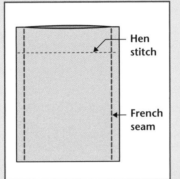
Hen stitch
French seam

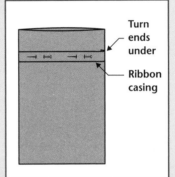
Turn ends under
Ribbon casing

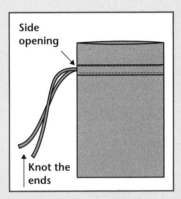
Side opening
Knot the ends

**1** Fold over 2 in [5 cm] on each end of the fabric and slip hem the turnings as shown on p. 21. Fold the hemmed fabric in half with the wrong sides facing.

**2** Make an encased seam on each side of the bag, following the instructions on p. 19. When the French seams are done, turn the bag right side out, ready to apply the ribbon casing to the outer surface.

**3** Cut the casing ribbon in half. Take one piece, turn raw ends under and pin across one side of the bag, concealing the line of hem stitches. Create a channel with small, even running stitches (p. 18) along each edge. Repeat and match with the remaining ribbon on the other side.

**4** There will be a narrow opening in the casing on either side of the bag, level with the side seams. Cut the drawstring ribbon or cord in half and use a bodkin or small safety pin to thread it right around the casing (see instructions opposite). Knot the ends together. With remaining ribbon or cord, repeat from the opposite side.

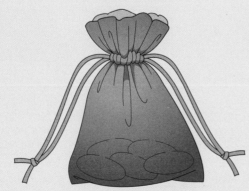

Place the favor inside the bag and draw up the ribbons or cord to close it. Before you fill the bag, you might like to trim it in various ways, with embroidery, lace or beads.

# BINDING

There are two main types of binding tape, although they are available in different materials, from heavy duty twill to nylon net.

## Straight tape

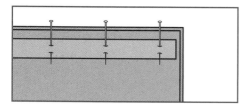

**1** Straight tape is used to reinforce the stitching on seams where there may be too much tension on the sewing thread alone, such as shoulders and waistbands. The tape is pinned over the stitch line so that the stitching will go through three layers all together.

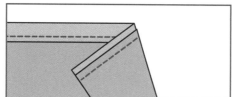

**2** When the seam is done, the seam allowance is trimmed back close to the stitch line without cutting into the tape.

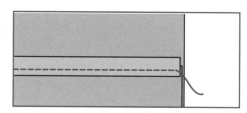

**3** Straight tape is also useful for turning hems. If the fabric is thick or fraying, sew tape around the right side of the raw edge and use it as the hemming edge.

## Bias binding

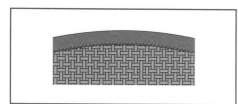

**1** Bias binding, as its name implies, is manufactured on the bias (p. 8) and follows the contours of any seam. It is used to encase fraying edges, particularly on thick fabrics and quilted items that cannot be neatened by turning.

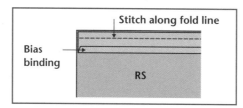

**2** Press one half of the bias binding open, align with the raw edge of the fabric on the *right* side and stitch along the fold line of the binding (for speed, if possible use a sewing machine for this).

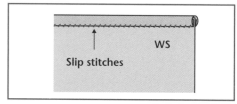

**3** Fold binding over the raw edge to meet the previous line of stitches on the wrong side. Slip stitch along fold of binding.

## Bias binding as decoration

Bias binding is frequently used decoratively and can be bought in many colors and patterns. It is made in satin as well as matt finish and in a range of widths. For true originality, make your own bias binding from any fabric so long as it is cut properly at an angle of 45 degrees to the grain. To use as double fold tape you must cut the strip four times the planned finished width.

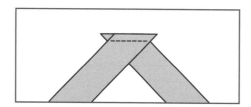

**1** Joining the strips is managed by stitching along the straight grain with the bias strips at a right angle. Press the seam flat open afterward.

**2** Binding the edge of a baby's bib not only solves the problem of hemming towelling fabric, but the binding can also be extended to form the neck ties.

# GATHERING AND PLEATING

Both gathers and pleats are designed to deal with the fullness of fabric.

## Gathers

Casings (p. 22) are an adjustable means of gathering—as is rufflette tape on curtains—but we need to fix gathers permanently too, for example on a gathered skirt or puffed sleeve.

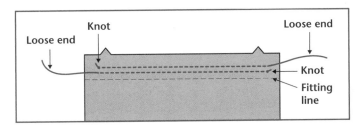

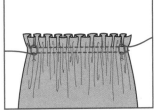

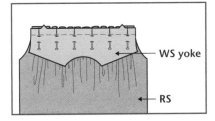

**1** Within the seam allowance of ⅝ in [1.5 cm], sew two lines of evenly spaced running stitch in opposite directions. Start each with a strong knot and leave the far end loose.

**2** The gathers will draw up when both loose ends are gently pulled at the same time. Wind each end around a pin to keep fabric to the desired width.

**3** Lay the gathers out flat and adjust if necessary before pinning on the yoke or waistband and basting ready for final stitching. This is the time to add straight tape reinforcement if required (see opposite).

## Pleats

Pleats regulate fullness in a more structured way than gathers. They need careful measurement and a lot of preparation in terms of pinning and basting. Have the steam iron ready because pleating demands that you press as you go.

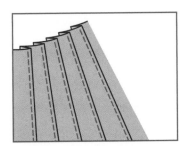

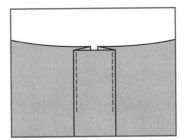

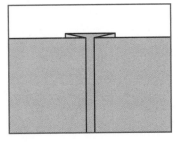

**1** A knife pleat is a simple fold in one direction only, either left or right. Pressing the pleats will set them but thicker fabrics are often edge stitched too, to keep a sharper outline.

**2** A box pleat is formed by two knife pleats facing opposite ways. These are usually top stitched to help maintain their shape around the hips.

**3** An inverted box pleat is made when the knife pleats point in toward each other. This is a common feature of pockets on military uniforms.

A kick pleat is a short, closed pleat, usually about 12 in [30 cm] long, at the hem of a straight skirt, usually at the back. It allows greater freedom of movement and must be reinforced at the top on either side to prevent tearing.

# SMOCKING

Smocking is a traditional form of hand embroidery, worked over small folds of evenly gathered fabric. When the gathering threads are removed the resulting fabric is quite stretchy, which is ideal for children's clothes. Smocking also looks good on the yoke area of blouses and around the cuffs of full sleeves, and it makes an attractive pocket detail. In the realms of home furnishings, panels of smocked silk, linen or velvet look luxurious on pillow covers. It takes extra fabric—on average allow three to four times the intended final width.

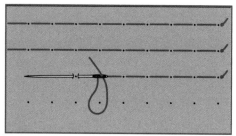

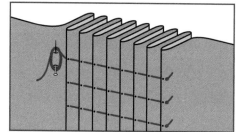

Now you can begin embroidering across the fronts of the folds. Standard six-strand embroidery floss is suitable—although you will work with only three strands at a time—and a crewel or embroidery needle (p. 6).

**1** Unless you are smocking a gingham or stripe, where the pattern provides a guide, you will have to iron a transfer of smocking dots on to the *wrong* side of your fabric and *with the grain*. Stitch between the dots as shown, using contrasting thread that will be easy to remove.

**2** Pull up the gathering threads—not too tightly—and tie in pairs or wrap around pins to keep your fabric to the desired width. Make sure the gathers are even.

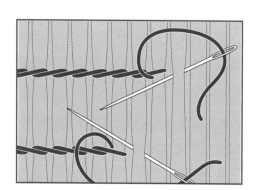

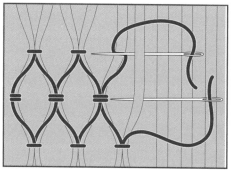

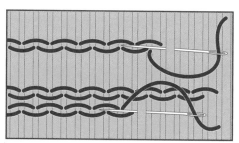

**1** **Stem stitch** Because smocking is meant to be fairly elastic, try not to work too tightly. Make your first row in this simple stitch to test and establish your tension.

**2** **Surface honeycomb stitch** Back stitch across two folds, needle out between them, go down ¼ in [6 mm] and enter the next right-hand fold from right to left. Make another back stitch at that point and repeat the sequence going up and down alternately. Repeat a line below, mirrorwise, to form the honeycomb pattern. Always check thread is correctly above or below needle.

**3** **Cable stitch** Needle out through first fold left, thread below needle and stitch over second fold, bringing needle out between first and second. Work with thread above and below needle alternately. Double cable stitch is two rows of cable worked together so they reflect each other.

# WAISTBANDS AND CUFFS

Waistbands have to be firm and so they are usually cut out in the warp direction (p. 8) parallel to the selvage. They can be supported by a very stiff tape like Petersham, which remains visible on the inside of the band. A flat skirt or trouser hook may be incorporated into the overlapping end, with a bar to match on the other end.

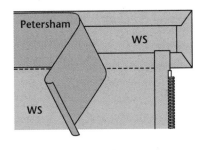

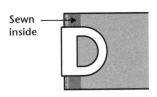

Alternatively, waistbands—and cuffs—can be strengthened internally with a material such as buckram or vilene. Some interfacings are iron-on, which can save you time but you should check machine washability.

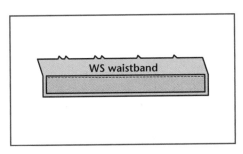

**1** Fold waistband in half lengthwise and stitch interfacing into position against center line.

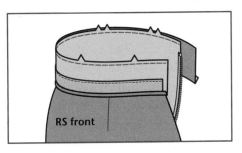

**2** Match pattern notches, pin and baste right sides together and firmly stitch waistband to skirt (if possible use a sewing machine for this). Press up the narrow turning below the interfacing.

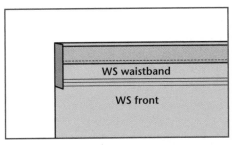

**3** Trim and layer seam allowances to reduce bulk before they are encased.

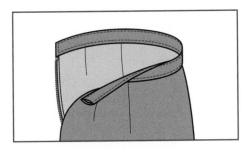

**4** Fold waistband along edge of interfacing so that pressed-up edge meets main stitch line. Pin, baste and hem to finish.

The hook-and-loop system of fastening known as Velcro needs very little pressure and is ideal for anybody who finds buttons and zippers difficult to manage. Velcro can be trimmed to size without fraying and sewn in position as required on cuffs and waistbands and plackets. Take care to seal all Velcro surfaces before putting in the washing machine.

# OPENINGS AND FASTENINGS

Below every waistband or collar lies the opening. The simplest kind is where the seam turnings are neatened with a tape insert. A more substantial opening contains a placket. This two-strip placket is neatly constructed from two pieces of fabric, one single and one folded double. It is an opening that could take a zipper (p. 41) just as easily as a row of buttons or a strip of Velcro. Note the topstitched reinforcement.

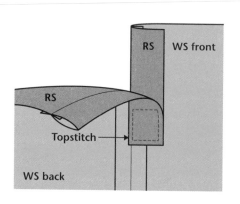

## Fastenings

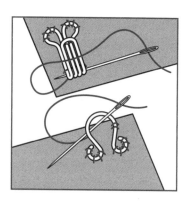

**1** Use one or two hook and eye combinations to fasten a waistband, depending on the width. Waistbands take a lot of stress, so work buttonhole stitch around the hook and eye attachments, with additional oversewing to prevent them loosening.

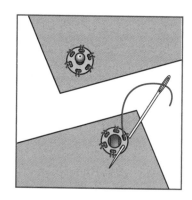

**2** Using all four holes, sew the stud half of the snap to the overlap so that it presses home more effectively. Don't let the stitches show on the right side. Line up the position for the lower half by running your needle through the center hole of the stud. If desired, sew a button on the right side of the overlap directly over the stud.

## Sewing on a coat button

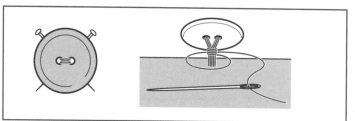

Use double sewing thread if you have no button thread. Buttons on coats and jackets should not be sewn tight against the cloth but should allow room for an extra layer when done up. Some buttons are manufactured with a shank but many are not. The thickness of two pins criss-crossed beneath the button will establish the shank's length and after a few stitches you can remove the pins and start to wind the thread around it. Finish with a row of buttonhole stitches for extra strength.

## Sewing a button loop

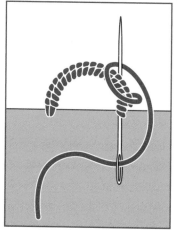

Loops make good alternative fastenings for clothes and bags. Sew them on the edge of one side, to align with a toggle or button on the other. Secure thread by oversewing, test for size with the button and loop across to a second fixing point. Continue looping to and fro several times before buttonhole stitching neatly to hold the strands together.

# MAKING A HAND-SEWN BUTTONHOLE

Once you know how many buttons you will be using, you must decide whether the buttonholes will run vertically or horizontally and how far from the edge. The answer depends on the direction of strain that the button(s) will take. If there is none, the holes can be made vertical, since the button does not need to move at all.

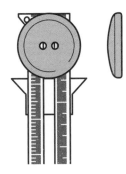

The finished buttonhole should not be over $\frac{1}{8}$ in [3 mm] longer than the button itself but you have to make an initial cut in the fabric. As a rule, add the width of the button to its thickness, plus the $\frac{1}{8}$ in [3 mm] for ease. Testing first on a spare scrap of fabric, mark the length with a pin at each end and baste or draw an accurate line between the two. Using very sharp embroidery scissors or a seam ripper, pierce the fabric mid-line and cut.

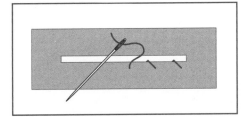

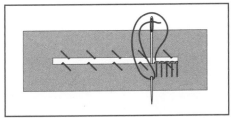

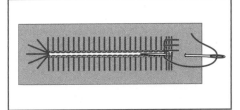

**1** Overcast the cut edges to prevent them fraying. Make four to six stitches down each side of the buttonhole. They should be about $\frac{1}{8}$ in [3 mm] deep.

**2** Hold the buttonhole as flat as possible while you are sewing. Buttonhole stitch is the same as blanket stitch (p. 18) but the stitches lie much closer together. Keep them the same depth for neatness.

**3** This style of buttonhole is called *fan and bar* due to the shapes the stitches make at either end. You may choose to make both ends the same. The bar is said to be stronger because of the two or three straight stitches that form the foundation for the buttonhole stitches that cover them. The fan is more attractive and consists of five graded stitches with the longest in line with the cut.

# ATTACHING SET-IN SLEEVES

There are many different styles of sleeve, for example (*from left to right*): raglan, dolman, bishop, puffed, tucked and tailored. Notice that neither raglan nor dolman styles have an over-shoulder seam—they are not set-in like the others.

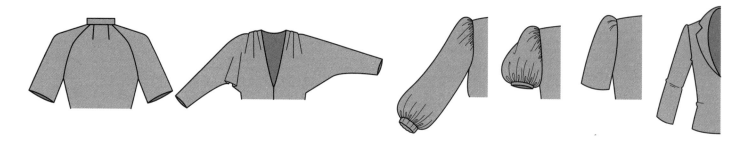

The set-in sleeve is joined to the main garment by a seam that goes all the way round the armhole. Whether gathered or tailored, the set-in sleeve demands the most preparation by hand, although the final stage is usually machine sewn. The process begins with cutting out and it is immediately obvious that the sleeve head is larger than the armhole for which it is intended. However, it is the cut of the sleeve head that enables the arm to move freely.

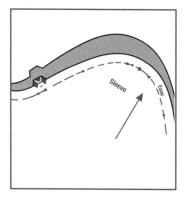

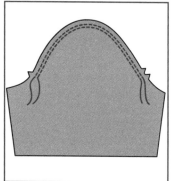

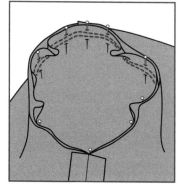

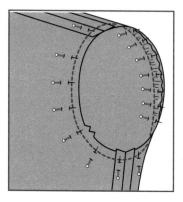

**1** The sleeve pattern has notches that correspond to those on the armhole of the main garment, and also markings to show the extent of the gathering line within the curve of the sleeve head.

**2** Sew a double line of running stitches along the gathering line, leaving the thread ends free. Afterward, join the sleeve seam, press it open and turn sleeve right side out.

**3** Pin the head into the armhole before pulling up to fit. Pull the gathers evenly and the head will smooth out. For a puffed sleeve rising above the shoulder seam, pull the outer line more than the inner one to make the sleeve head arch over.

**4** Distribute the gathers evenly, but *do not cut away any excess fabric yet*. Baste firmly and remove the pins before trying the garment on. Now is the time for any alterations. A tailored sleeve should be smooth-fitting with no puckering on the right side. After final stitching, neaten armhole by oversewing or binding.

# TRIMMING: BEADS, SEQUINS AND BOWS

## Beads

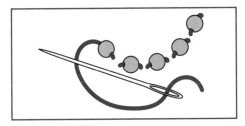 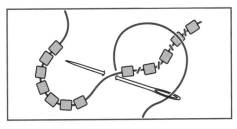 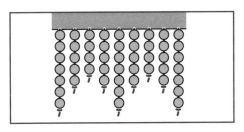

Choose the correct size and shape of beads for your design and work with a fine needle. Secure thread, bring needle through and thread on one bead. Insert needle back into or near the same hole. Advance one stitch on wrong side and bring needle through ready for next bead.

Thread up two needles and secure both threads on the wrong side. Bring first needle through and thread with desired number of beads. With second needle, stitch over the first thread coming through the first bead; this is *couching*. Slide the second bead close to the first and repeat until all beads are in place.

For a bead fringe, tie first (anchor) bead on to thread and knot firmly. Add as many beads as desired, securing thread with two small stitches on the fabric edge before finishing off. Start a new strand in the same way, next to the first.

## Sequins

  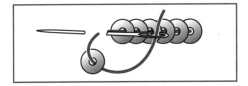

Secure thread on wrong side and bring needle up through eye of first sequin. Back stitch over the right hand edge, come out on the left hand edge and back stitch down through the eye. Advance a stitch and repeat with next sequin.

Secure thread on wrong side and bring needle up through eye of first sequin. Thread on one small bead before re-inserting needle through same eye. Pull firmly to bring bead in contact with sequin. Advance one stitch on wrong side and bring needle up through eye of next sequin.

To overlap sequins, secure thread on wrong side and bring needle up through eye of first sequin. Needle in on left hand edge and up again at distance of half a sequin. Thread second sequin on and back stitch to edge of first one. Advance one stitch on wrong side and bring needle up again at distance of half a sequin. Each new sequin covers the eye of the previous one.

## Flat ribbon bow

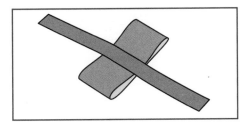  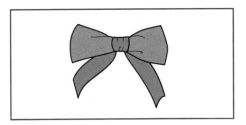

**1** Take two lengths of ribbon, one wide and one narrow. Loosely fold the wide one into a rectangle with ends overlapping halfway down the longer side. Join three layers together with a small cross stitch and lay the narrow ribbon across at right angles.

**2** Turn both ribbons over and tie the narrow one in a knot that will pinch the wide ribbon into a bow shape.

**3** Turn the ribbons right side up. Pull both ends of the narrow ribbon so they hang on one side of the wide one. Trim level.

# PROJECT: APRON

This apron has a large double pocket, useful for cooks, gardeners and craftspeople. Make it from any close woven, pre-shrunk fabric like canvas, denim, calico or gingham.

Make a paper pattern by ruling a large sheet of paper with a grid of 2 in [5 cm] squares. Scale up the pieces, square by square, from the grid below; a ⅝ in [1.5 cm] seam allowance has been included all round. Cut out the paper shapes and pin to the fabric; remember to place the center of the main piece on a fold. Cut out the fabric and remove the paper.

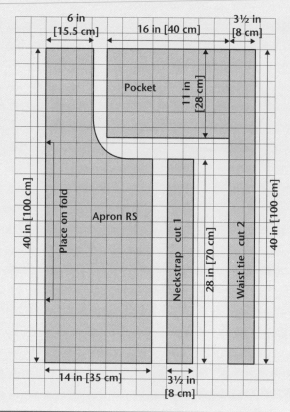

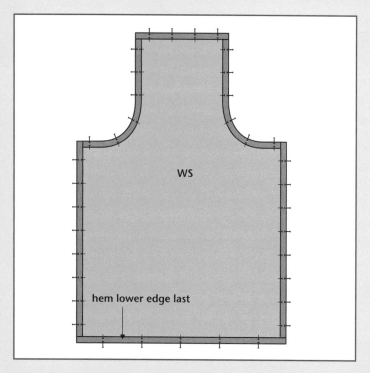

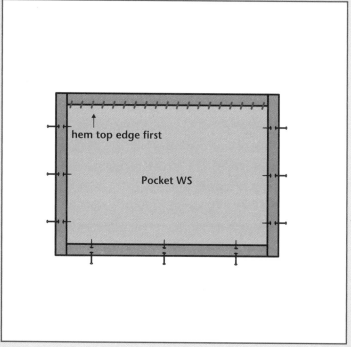

**1** Fold over and pin ⅝ in [1.5 cm] in a neat hem around the main piece; clip the waistline curves for a smooth turning. Baste and then machine or hem stitch right round, finishing along the lower edge. Press.

**2** Hem the top of the pocket piece. With a single fold, baste down the seam allowance on the other three sides. Press. If you like, add an appliquéd or embroidered design to the pocket at this stage.

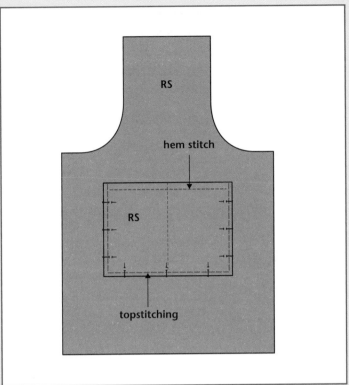

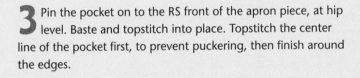

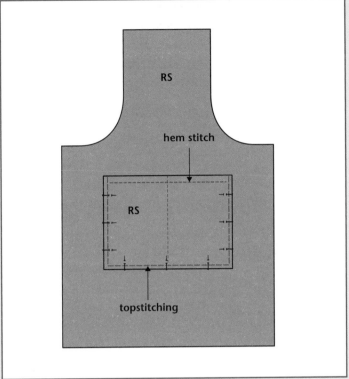

**4** Fold the neck strap and waist ties in half lengthwise, RS together. Stitch one end and the side seams on all three, as shown. Clip the points and corners, turn RS out and press.

**3** Pin the pocket on to the RS front of the apron piece, at hip level. Baste and topstitch into place. Topstitch the center line of the pocket first, to prevent puckering, then finish around the edges.

**5** For an adjustable neck strap, make three buttonholes. Turn in the raw end of the strap and neaten by oversewing. Attach it to one corner of the apron top with reinforced stitching, as shown. Sew a button to the other corner. Alternatively, you may make one buttonhole in the apron top and sew three buttons to the strap.

**6** Finish the waist ties in the same way as the neck strap, minus the buttonholes.

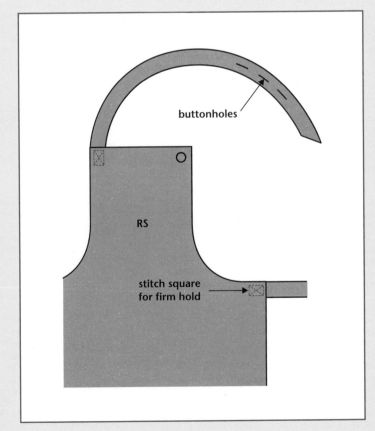

# TRIMMING: EDGINGS, ROULEAU AND APPLIQUÉ

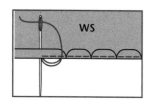

**Shell edging**
Fold or roll
and tack a
narrow double
turning. Make
a decorative
hem with three running stitches followed
by a vertical loop up over the edge. Pull
tight to form the scallop. If necessary, make
two vertical stitches, depending on fabric
thickness.

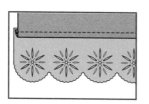

**Lace edging**
Baste a narrow
turning, then
pin and baste
a length of
gathered
lace behind the fold. Sew all three layers
together with neat running or back stitch;
alternatively, use a straight machine stitch.

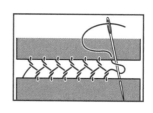

**Faggoting** Lay
lace parallel
to fabric and
baste both
onto backing
paper. Bring
needle through lower edge and insert into
top edge from back to front a little to the
right. Twist needle under and over thread
across the gap, then insert into lower edge
from back to front, again to the right.
Repeat to the end, remove paper.

## Rouleau

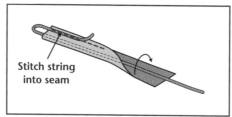

Stitch string
into seam

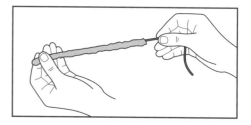

**1** Rouleau is constructed from bias strips
(p. 24). It is used to make spaghetti
straps; stitched-down designs on lapels and
bodices; and wired trimmings for hats and
bridal head-dresses.

**2** Fold bias strips right sides together,
and sew to the required width. Stretch
fabric slightly as you go so it won't strain
the thread later. Include a length of thin
string, longer than the tube, at the top
of the seam and push the free end down
inside. Finish stitching the seam.

**3** Trim the seam allowance to $^1/_8$–$^1/_4$ in
[3–6 mm]. Pull on the string to turn
the tube right side out. Pull slowly at first
until you feel the fabric coming through.

## Appliqué

**1** Appliqué is
cut-out fabric
decoration attached
to a base by stitching
around the shapes. It
is used in dressmaking
and home furnishings,
especially quilts. First cut out pieces with a small seam allowance,
snip any curves (p. 19) and pin or baste them to the base fabric,
with guidelines if necessary.

**2** With a straw needle, stitch
down the shapes, turning
the raw edges in with the
needle as you go; use hemming
(p. 21) or blanket stitch (p. 18).
Appliqué by machine offers a
wide choice of stitch effects.

**3** Remove pins and basting
when you have finished.
Press your appliqué lightly,
face down on a well-padded
surface like a towel, so the seam
allowances don't show through
on the front.

# PART THREE:
# MACHINE SEWING METHODS AND TECHNIQUES

## THREADING THE SEWING MACHINE

Newer-style sewing machines incorporate the tension discs, thread guides and take-up lever inside their casings, eliminating various steps involved with threading the older models. We include both because many older machines are still in use (see also pp. 10–11). Always *consult the manufacturer's manual* but here are general instructions for preparing the top thread on a sewing machine.

**1** Lift the presser foot to release tension discs and allow thread to run easily.

**2** Raise needle as far as possible by turning the hand/balance wheel.

**3** Place a spool of thread on the spool pin and pull the free end into the first thread guide.

**4** On new-style machines, take thread around the auto tension channel and down to the thread guide just above the needle. On older models, thread around the tension dial and snap up through the tension wire.

**5** Older models also operate with a prominent take-up lever. Pass the thread through the eye of this lever and then down to the thread guide just above the needle.

**6** Now thread the needle. Be aware that some thread from front to back and some from left to right. Look for the groove above the eye where the thread runs during stitching. Finally, pull through a good working length of thread, about 6 in [15 cm].

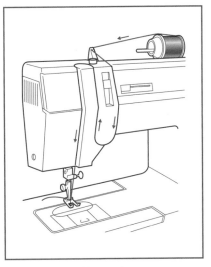

**New style**

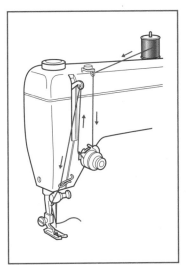

**Old style**

Incorrect threading is probably responsible for more beginners' problems than any other factor. If you have no book of instructions, search for your make and model on the internet, where a huge range of manuals is available.

# THE BOBBIN

The bobbin holds the lower thread on a sewing machine. It lies next to the needle plate, in a compartment with a sliding lid. Lower thread tension is controlled by a small screw that regulates the spring on the bobbin case. Some bobbins operate clockwise and others counterclockwise—once again, *consult the manufacturer's manual.*

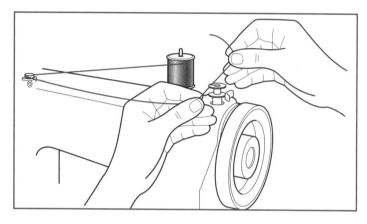

The bobbin is filled automatically from the winder on the machine, which ensures it is evenly wound under tension. Some bobbins can be filled in situ under the plate.

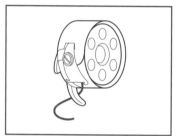

This type sits vertically in the bobbin chase and is released by a latch on the case. When replaced, the thread should slot under the spring with a tail of 4 in [10 cm].

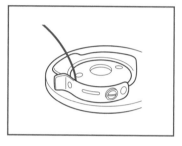

The drop-in type sits horizontally beneath the lid. There is usually an angled slot to pull the bobbin thread through.

# THE IMPORTANCE OF TENSION

The machine stitch is formed by the top and lower threads interlocking in the fabric.

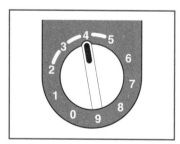

**1** Top thread tension is governed by the tension dial, numbered 0–9. Behind it, the thread runs between two or three discs that are adjusted according to the dial.

**2** Between 4 and 5 on the dial is considered normal tension. The threads meet in the center of the fabric and the stitching appears the same on each side.

**3** Below 4, the tension discs loosen and the top thread runs more freely. The thread can then pass through both layers of fabric. This is only desirable if you want to create gathers by pulling up the bottom thread.

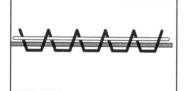

**4** Above 5, the discs are screwed together more tightly and the reverse happens.

# TROUBLESHOOTING

| PROBLEM | REASON | REMEDY |
|---|---|---|
| Machine does not sew | Power switch is turned off | Turn on the switch |
| Bobbin winder is engaged | | Disengage bobbin winder |
| Fabric does not move | Presser foot is not lowered | Lower presser foot |
| Machine skips stitches | Machine is not threaded correctly | Re-thread correctly |
| Needle blunt or loose | | Change needle and tighten |
| Needle unthreads | Needle wrong way round | Set needle correctly |
| Needle breaks | Bent needle | Change needle. Raise needle when removing work |
| Stitches are irregular | Needle size is not correct for thread and fabric | Use appropriate needle |
| Machine is not threaded correctly | | Re-thread correctly |
| Top thread tension is too loose | | Adjust tension |
| Fabric is being pulled or pushed against machine | | Guide gently with feeding action |
| Puckered seams | Tension too tight or needle wrong way round | Loosen top tension or set needle correctly |
| Thread breaks | Tension too tight or needle wrong way round | Loosen top tension or set needle correctly |
| Snagged fabric | Bent or blunt needle | Change needle |
| Thread bunches | Top bobbin threads are not drawn back under | Draw both threads back under presser foot before starting seam about 6 in [10 cm] and hold until a few stitches are formed |
| Bobbin thread breaks | Bobbin case is not threaded correctly | Check bobbin is rotating in the right direction |
| Lint accumulates in bobbin case or hook | | Remove lint |
| Tangled bobbin thread | Bobbin wound too loosely or inserted wrongly | Do not wind bobbins by hand. Check bobbin unwinds in the right direction |

# STITCH LENGTH

Stitch length is now measured in millimeters from 1 to 6 and controlled by a dial or lever (pp. 10–11). This activates the feed dogs, which in turn move fabric the required distance under the pressure foot (p. 12).

Use the longest stitches (4–6 mm [¹/₈–¼ in]) for heavyweight fabrics, topstitching, gathering and basting. Medium length stitches (2.5–4 mm [³/₃₂–¹/₈ in]) are suitable for mid-weight fabrics. Fine fabrics use a 2 mm [¹/₁₆ in] stitch. A row of 1 mm [¹/₃₂ in] stitches is difficult to undo, so it pays to be sure of what you are doing when using them.

# STITCH WIDTH

Stitch width does not apply to straight stitching. The width control (pp. 10–11) sets the swing of the needle when working zigzag or other decorative stitches. Again, the measurement is in millimeters and usually goes up to 6 mm [¼ in].

# MACHINING SPECIAL FABRICS

A number of fabrics have special sewing requirements, particularly where needles are concerned.

**Sheer fabrics** like voile, organdie, batiste or chiffon look best with encased seams that don't detract from their delicate appearance. Remove selvages first to prevent puckering. The main problem lies with sheers being so thin and slippery to handle. Practice will help; take an offcut and run up a sample seam using the correct (new) needle and thread. The recommended needle size is 8–11, with a fine cotton or polyester thread and a stitch length of 1.5–2 mm [approx ¹/₁₆ in]. A single-hole needle plate can help to stabilize the fabric surface as the needle punches through. You can also try sewing with tissue paper under the fabric.

**Denim** looks tough enough in a finished garment but it frays easily and—like sheer fabrics—requires encased seams. Use an 11–14 needle.

**Velvets**, due to the pile, can be as difficult as sheer fabrics and undoing stitches from velvet leaves marks. Basting should consist of short stitches with the occasional back stitch. On the machine, velvet takes a stitch length of 2–2.5 mm [approx ¹/₁₆ in] with a loosened thread tension, using an 11–14 needle.

Once again, practice on offcuts. If the velvet layers shift about, baste *and* pin firmly in the seam allowance before you begin. As you stitch, hold the bottom layer taut without dragging on the needle. Remove the pins as you go.

**Knits** must be handled with care while machining, as it is all too easy to stretch them out of shape. Work at a gentle speed and remember that your seams need to give a little with the natural stretch of jersey fabric. Change your regular needle to an 11–14 ballpoint that won't split the fibers as it sews. Use the stretch stitch on your machine, if you have it, or the tricot. Otherwise, try zigzag on the narrowest setting. Knits do not unravel so seam finishing is not necessary. However, you may feel that certain seams— shoulders and waists, for example—could benefit from being taped (p. 24).

**Stretching seam**

**Seam stretched in wear**

# MACHINING AN ENCASED SEAM

The sequence for machining a French seam is the same as it is for hand sewing (p. 19).

## The flat fell seam

Sometimes called run and fel', this is another type of encased seam, widely used for tough-wearing casual clothes, skirts, pants, jeans and fabric bags. It is completely reversible with two visible rows of stitching on each side.

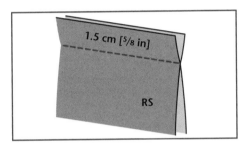

**1** Pin wrong sides together and stitch with a ⅝ in [1.5 cm] seam allowance.

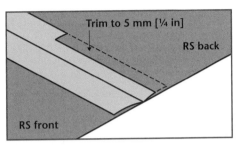

**2** Press open and trim one side of the allowance to ¼ in [5 mm].

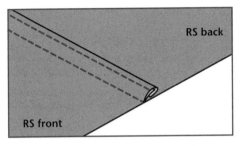

**3** Fold uncut seam allowance in half, press and fold over to enclose previously cut edge. Pin, baste and machine along fold.

# MACHINED SEAM FINISHES

The sequence for machining a bias binding is the same as it is for hand sewing (p. 24), except that the final slip stitch (Step 3) may be replaced by machine stitching too. Here are some other solutions to seam finishing.

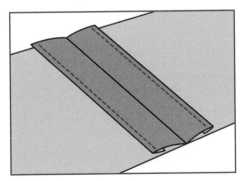

**Edge stitched** Stitch ⅛–¼ in [3–6 mm] from the raw edge on each side. Fold over on the stitch line and stitch close to the edge of the fold.

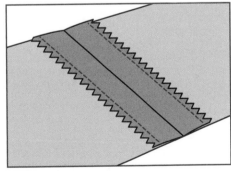

**Stitched and pinked** A finish for close-woven fabrics that prevents curling. Stitch to ¼ in [6 mm] from the edge of each seam allowance. Trim close to stitching with pinking shears.

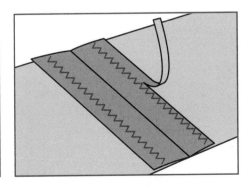

**Zigzagged and trimmed** Zigzag stitch down the edge of each allowance on the widest stitch setting but do not stitch over the edge. Trim close to stitching with shears.

# MAKING DARTS

Darts give shape to flat fabric and enable it to fit over curved contours, for example on the bodice of a dress or the back of an armchair. They are marked by small dots on a paper pattern and are transferred to the fabric at the cutting-out stage with a fabric marker or tailor's chalk.

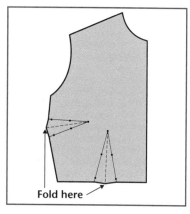

**Fold here**

**1** Match pattern dots together by folding down the center. You will see that the stitch line will eventually form a triangle.

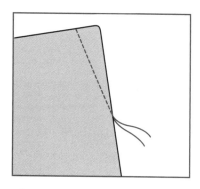

**2** Pin, baste and machine the dart to a sharp point by stitching past the edge of the fabric. Raise presser foot and cut threads, leaving sufficient length to finish neatly by hand.

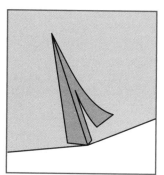

**3** Darts in lightweight fabrics do not usually need trimming. Simply press the folded edge of the dart to one side without creasing the main fabric. Darts in thick fabric should be cut open on the fold and trimmed back before pressing.

# SHAPED FACINGS

Facings are used to neaten the edges of necklines and armholes and are cut to the same shape and, most importantly, *on the same grain or bias* as the main garment. They can be stiffened a little with an interfacing if required, sewn or ironed on to the facing itself. It is easier to edge stitch or trim the outer edges of the facings with pinking shears before attaching.

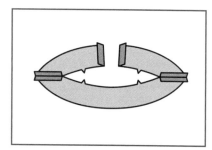

**1** The facing for a neckline, showing the joins between front and back sections, and the ends turned back where they are to meet the fastening on the main piece.

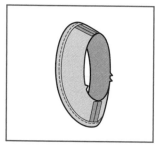

**2** The facing for an armhole prepared with edge stitching.

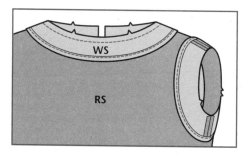

WS

RS

**3** The facings attached to the main garment, ready for the curved seams to be clipped (p. 19) and turned right side out.

# INSERTING A ZIPPER

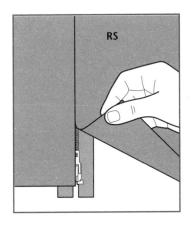

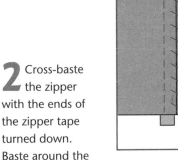

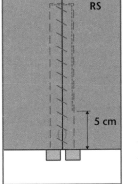

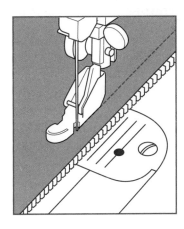

**1** Set the zipper into the seam in the closed position. The fabric edges should meet at the center and conceal the teeth.

**2** Cross-baste the zipper with the ends of the zipper tape turned down. Baste around the stitch line as well, passing about 1 in [2.5 cm] clear of the end of the zipper teeth. Start machining 2 in [5 cm] below the zipper head in order to keep a straight line.

**3** Topstitch around the zipper using the zipper foot to run close to the edge of the opening. Stop 2 in [5 cm] short of the zipper head on the other side and, removing the cross-basting, slide the zipper head down in order to complete the stitching at both sides of the top.

# TOPSTITCHING

Topstitching can be used for purely decorative purposes and is frequently done in a contrasting color around lapels and pockets. Use a longer stitch than you would for ordinary seam sewing.

# MACHINING A BUTTONHOLE

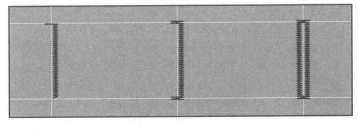

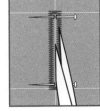

**2** Pierce the center of the buttonhole with embroidery scissors or a seam ripper and cut open carefully from end to end without clipping the bars.

**1** Mark the desired position of the buttonhole(s) with a fabric marker or tailor's chalk. Using a zigzag machine foot, set the stitch selector and make a few stitches to form the bar of the buttonhole before travelling steadily down the first side. Make the second bar at the bottom and then turn the fabric through 180 degrees to complete the other side.

# SHIRRING

Shirring looks very like smocking without the embroidery. It is ideal for nightwear and beachwear. Shirring elastic is specially manufactured for use in sewing machines and is easier to apply than stitching down flat elastic. As with all techniques that you try for the first time, it is advisable to practice on an offcut before sewing your main piece.

**1** Fill your bobbin by hand with shirring elastic and load it into your machine as usual. Adjust the thread tension to 4 and change from straight stitch to the longest, widest zigzag that your settings will allow.

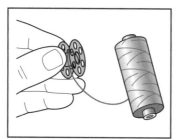

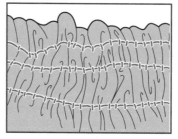

**2** You will need to complete three or four rows before achieving the smocked effect. This shows the wrong side.

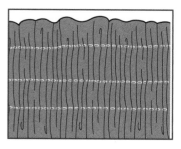

**3** And this is the right side. Shirring works equally well on plain and patterned fabrics.

# MAKING CORDING

Cording makes a smart external seam finish for clothes and home furnishings. The cord should be pre-shrunk; check when buying. It comes in various thicknesses, so use whatever is appropriate for your fabric. Cording needs to be supple and bend around corners so it is encased in bias-cut strips (p. 24).

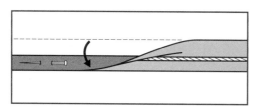

**1** Pin the cord into the fabric and baste, leaving a normal seam allowance.

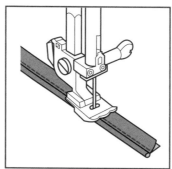

**2** Use a cording foot for best results, although a zipper foot performs well too. Stitch as close as possible to the cord. You can produce a continuous strip of piping to be cut up and used as required.

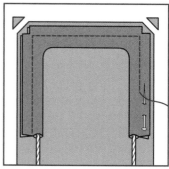

**3** Alternatively, pin the piping in place and baste it to shape before machining. If turnings are bulky, layer them and cut off the excess to give neatly turned corners.

# PROJECT: DACHSHUND DRAFT EXCLUDER

A faithful dog with floppy ears to guard you against drafts—and he can fit across any door simply by adjusting the length between his head and tail.

Any type of fabric is suitable, including knits. Make a paper pattern by ruling a large sheet of paper with a grid of 3 ½ in [9 cm] squares. Scale up the pieces, square by square, from the grid below. Cut out the paper templates and pin to the fabric, noting which pieces must go on a fold. *When cutting out the fabric add a ½ in [12 mm] seam allowance all round.*

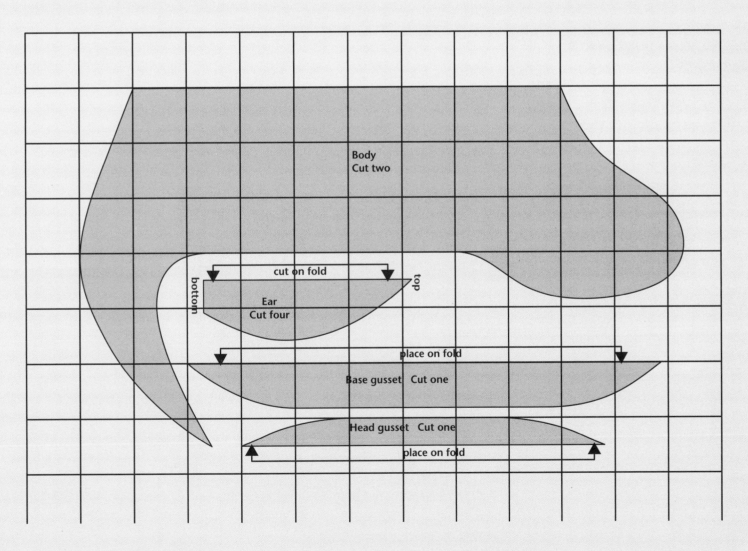

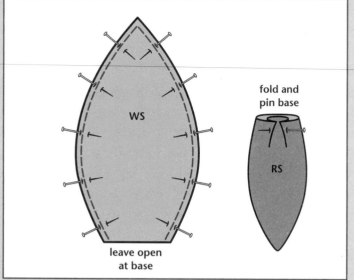

fold and
pin base

WS

RS

leave open
at base

WS

finished
ear

RS body

head
gusset

**1** To make a pair of ears, pin each pair of shapes RS facing and stitch right round except for the base. Turn RS out. Fold, pin and baste a small pleat in each.

**2** On the RS of one half of the main body, pin and firmly baste the head gusset as shown, stitching one of the finished ears between the two layers of fabric. Repeat with the other half of the body and the second ear.

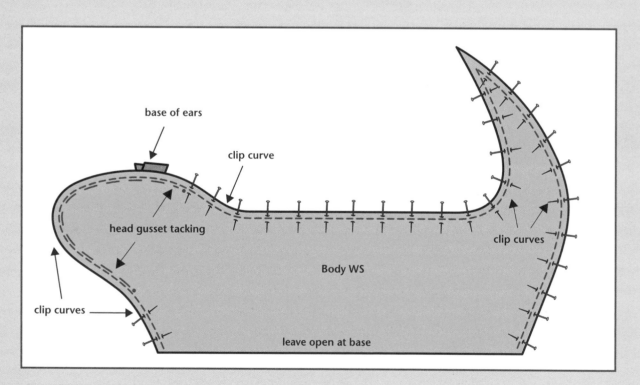

base of ears

clip curve

head gusset tacking

Body WS

clip curves

clip curves

leave open at base

**3** RS facing, with the ear flaps safely clear of the needle, machine stitch each half of the dog's head to its own side of the head gusset.

**4** Machine stitch the remaining halves of the body together from chin to base, and from neck up to tip of tail and down the other side. Leave the base itself open. Clip curves in preparation for turning. Remove all basting.

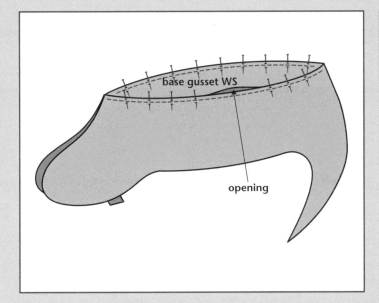

**5** Still WS out, fit the base gusset as shown. Machine stitch around both sides of the body, leaving an opening of 4–5 in [10–12 cm] for stuffing.

**6** Turn the dog RS out and use a knitting needle to push his tail to a fine point. Stuff the head and body as firmly as you can with polyester toy filling. You may need a good deal, depending on his length.

**7** Close the raw edges of the opening and oversew.

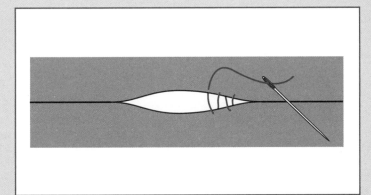

**8** Use buttons, felt appliqué or embroidery for the dog's eyes, nose and mouth, giving him a unique personality. Fix a collar or bow around his neck as a finishing touch.

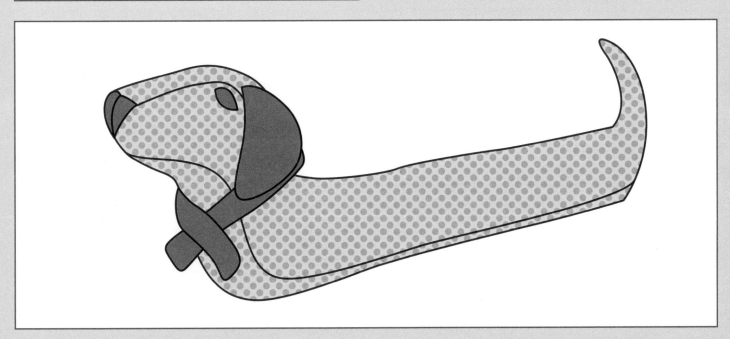

# LAUNDRY AND AFTERCARE

## LAUNDERING

Always look for the care symbols on any fabric that you buy; the manufacturer's care label appears on the bolt itself and you should also ask the shop assistant for a care ticket to take away with your purchase. This is useful to keep as part of a record of everything that you make. Other points of reference are your own washing machine and dryer manuals. These contain details of all the washing and drying programs, indicating how they tie in with the standard care symbols.

If possible, deal quickly with stains. Don't rub the affected area too hard because friction can damage the fibers and leave an obvious patch. Oil-based marks should be tackled from the wrong side of the fabric with a proper solvent; follow the manufacturer's instructions.

Whether washing by hand or machine, do not use washing powder on fabrics with a high wool or silk content. Instead, choose a liquid laundry detergent for delicate fabrics. The cleansing agents in liquid soaps are designed to work at low temperatures and won't leave a powdery deposit. Test strong colors (especially reds) for colorfastness and if in any doubt wash them separately. Woolen or wool-mix fabrics of any kind should always be rinsed in warm water. Use the machine-washable wool setting on your machine, not the low-temperature or hand-wash program that delivers a cold rinse.

Tumble dryers are large contributors to accidental shrinkage, and some fabrics are better left to dry without heat. Lift woolens from the washing machine and roll in a clean towel to remove excess water. Lay any knit fabrics, including jersey, to dry flat on a drying rack. Do not peg them up because they could lose shape as the moisture drains downward.

Iron fabrics according to the recommended heat setting. Take extra care if you have added trimmings. Nylon lace, metallic threads and plastic sequins will shrivel at the touch of a hot iron.

"Pressing" is often substituted for "ironing" but more strictly it means using steam and a pressing cloth. It is important to lift the iron straight up and down and avoid pulling it across the fabric when steam pressing. Make use of your sleeveboard, roll or tailor's ham (p. 5) to smooth awkward surfaces and contours.

## AFTERCARE

After all your effort, it's worth investing in good quality hangers for the clothes that you make. Sew hanging loops inside shoulder seams and waistbands to make sure garments are properly supported, not drooping in deep folds from a distorted shoulder line. Evening dresses and other delicate fabrics should hang inside protective covers to keep them clear of the floor and free from too much handling.

When placing clothes and household linen in storage, the golden rule is always to put items away clean, absolutely dry, and unstarched (silverfish love to eat starch). Dust, dirt and perspiration can harm and discolor fibers of all kinds—synthetics as well as natural—and both moths and molds feed readily on dirt.

Precious heirlooms like christening and wedding gowns should be laundered or dry cleaned, then layered with plenty of acid-free tissue paper and stored in zipped cotton cases. Keep curtains, loose covers and bed quilts folded neatly and well-protected in chests and cupboards, or inside zipped covers and lidded plastic boxes for long-term storage. Shake them out occasionally and refold a different way—this will prevent permanent creases from setting in.

Avoid the risk of mold or mildew by never storing fabrics in poorly ventilated, damp or humid surroundings such as lofts, cellars or seldom-opened cupboards. Low-powered heaters and dehumidifiers can help to reduce problems caused by dampness and condensation.

Stay vigilant for the tiny clothes moth. It has a life cycle of around six weeks, and it is the larvae that make ruinous holes in things. Today, there are pleasantly scented alternatives to camphor mothballs, such as cedarwood blocks and lavender bags, although these need renewing from time to time. Moths not only lay their eggs on woolen fibers but can also damage silk, fur or feathers. It is a wise precaution to check your storage places every so often; keep disturbing the moths' potential habitat and they won't settle.

# SEWING TERMS

**Appliqué**   The technique of stitching one fabric on top of another

**Basting (Tacking)**   Temporary stitches made with running stitch about 1/2 in [1.5 cm] long

**Bias**   Any diagonal line between lengthwise and crosswise grains. True bias, at 45 degrees to the selvage, gives maximum stretch

**Bias binding**   Binding strip cut on the bias to fit smoothly around curves without adding bulk. Purchase readymade, or cut from the fabric in hand to make a self bias binding

**Binding**   A narrow strip of fabric or tape used to cover the raw edges of a garment. It can be hidden on the inside or sewn on the surface as decoration

**Blind hemming**   Hem stitches that attach a folded edge virtually invisibly to a flat surface

**Calico**   Closely woven cotton fabric in a natural cream color. (the same name is often used for printed cotton fabrics)

**Casing**   A tube designed to contain elastic, cord, ribbon etc.

**Cording**   Gives a neat firm finish to a seam, especially on soft furnishings. The cord should be pre-shrunk and encased in bias-cut strips

**Dart**   A sewn structure that takes in fabric to give shape to a garment

**Ease**   The adjustable difference between body measurement and paper pattern, especially used for setting sleeves in an armhole

**Facing**   Shaped piece of fabric (frequently interfaced) enclosing raw edges inside a sleeve or neck opening

**Fusible web**   A synthetic material that bonds to fabric when melted by the heat of an iron

**Gathers**   Small folds gathered by drawing up a line of stitching. Used to create ruffles

**Grain line**   The direction in which the warp and weft threads lie. The warp running lengthwise, parallel to the selvage, is the lengthwise grain. The weft follows the crosswise grain, at right angles to the selvage

**Hem**   The turned-up area at the bottom of a garment, which prevents fraying

**Interfacing**   Extra fabric sewn or ironed between the layers of fabric to give it more body

**Lining**   A lightweight fabric (often taffeta or satin) sewn inside a garment to conceal seam allowances. Linings also block see-through in a lightweight fabric

**Loom state**   As the fabric comes off the loom, before it has undergone any further process. Loom state cloth will shrink

**Muslin**   A translucent loose-woven cotton fabric

**Nap**   Texture or design that runs in one direction only and influences pattern cutting layouts. With nap fabrics include velvet, corduroy and satin

**Notches**   Diamond-shaped marks that project beyond the pattern edge, for aligning pattern pieces at the sewing stage

**Notions**   Incidental items such as thread, fastenings, tape and trimmings

**Petersham**   Corded ribbon (similar to grosgrain) used to stiffen waistbands and also in millinery

**Pile**   The soft raised surface on velvet, corduroy and some brushed fabrics. It usually has a nap that can affect the color and influences pattern cutting layouts

**Pleat**   Folds controlling fabric fullness. Variations include box, inverted and knife pleats

**Pre-shrunk**   Fabric subjected to a shrinking process during manufacture

**Pressing**   Often used for ironing but more strictly means using steam and a pressing cloth

**RS**   Abbreviation for Right Side

**Raw edge**   Untreated cut edge of a piece of fabric, which may fray or unravel

**Rise**   Distance from crotch seam to waistband on pants

**Rouleau**   Narrow tubing constructed from bias strips, used for shoulder straps and applied decoration

**Seam**   Two pieces of fabric joined with a line of stitches. Variations include open, encased, French and flat fell seams

**Seam allowance**   Distance between the cut edge and the seam line

**Selvage**   The solid edge of a woven fabric

**Slip stitch**   Stitches that attach a folded edge virtually invisibly to a flat surface

**Snaps (Poppers)**   Press stud fastenings

**Stay stitching**   A line of straight stitches that prevents curved or bias edges, such as necklines, shoulders and waistlines, from stretching out of shape during sewing

**Tacking [Basting]**   Temporary stitches made with running stitch about 1/2 in [1.5 cm] long

**Tailor's tacks**   Temporary loops of thread for matching points or marking the position of darts or pockets

**Topstitching**   An extra row of stitching (usually decorative) done in matching or contrasting thread along or near a finished edge

**WS**   Abbreviation for Wrong Side

**Warp**   Runs lengthwise, parallel to the selvage, usually stronger than the weft

**Weft**   Runs at right angles to the selvage, not usually quite as strong as the warp